Bonfires

&

Other Vigils

Praise for
Bonfires & Other Vigils

There is an imperturbable sense of awe running through Bonfires & Other Vigils that settles dynamically between resolute observation and self-assured humility. The pieces offered here occupy poetry's sweet spot, where the speaker's personal vantage opens to the immediate familiarity of the universal. Colleen Alles presents her readers with everyday details—a used up wick, a broken eggshell, a mantis—that evoke the possibilities and confounding particulars of being creaturely: regret, confusion, joy, enchantment. In a world that moves at a tremendous clip, Alles invites us to be at home in her clamor of experiences and losses through naming them exactly, but without succumbing to the traps of domestication or malaise. It's a pleasure to have the door of experience held open by a poet so hospitable and keen-eyed: read this collection with slow and steady attention so you don't miss a single moment, even the smallest of chances to see the world anew.

- Dave Harrity, author of *These Intricacies and Our Father in the Year of the Wolf*

There's a sturdy house, a street, a garden, a neighborhood with dark and bright weathers, and a family of human and other lively creatures in these beautifully nuanced poems that invite us to see the largest of ideas in the small and holy domesticities: the fragility of a broken robin's egg, the all-seeing eyes of a praying mantis, and the vulnerability and resilience invoked by the threat of this broken world. These are tender home-loving poems that comfort the longings of the heart and satisfy the ear with quiet and precise lyricism.

- Anne-Marie Oomen, author of, *As Long As I Know You: the Mom Book,* winner AWP nonfiction award, and Michigan Author Award 2023-24.

Colleen's poems live close to the morning. They come alive the third moment after dawn and they follow you around all day, tap you on the shoulder, remind you to pay attention: to the seasonal road, to the polka dot bathing suit, to the scurry of squirrels. And like any good mother, Colleen's poems take care of you. They tuck you in at night, hold you against the faithless hours, tell you they're glad you're safe, how grateful they are that you're still here. I can say that I'm grateful, too, for these beautiful poems.

- Garrett Stack, author of *Yeoman's Work*

"At the river I found a beautiful place / to be wrong." In the face of anxieties at home and in the world, Bonfires & Other Vigils doesn't seek escape or a single, right answer. Instead, these poems are "content to keep waiting" and offer readers a down-to-earth way of paying attention. Alles' writing honors the tender markers of family life, neighborhoods, and home. These poems ask you to remember the ground right under your feet, working at the level of earthworm and grouse, dandelion and hound, tree rings and a daughter's curls. Here, a vigil isn't just about hoping for something different or praying toward a desired outcome. This collection shows how sometimes the best vigil is a refusal: "the letter I wrote / but didn't send... the naked body I saw... / but didn't resolve / to change."

- Emily Stoddard, author of *Divination with a Human Heart Attached*

Paperback: 979-8-9879562-5-0
Ebook: 979-8-9879562-8-1

First paperback edition April 2024
Cover design: Anna Luis

Printed by Mixam in the United States of America.

Red Rook Press
Box 870244
The University of Alabama
Tuscaloosa, AL 35487-0244

redrookpress.org

Bonfires & Other Vigils

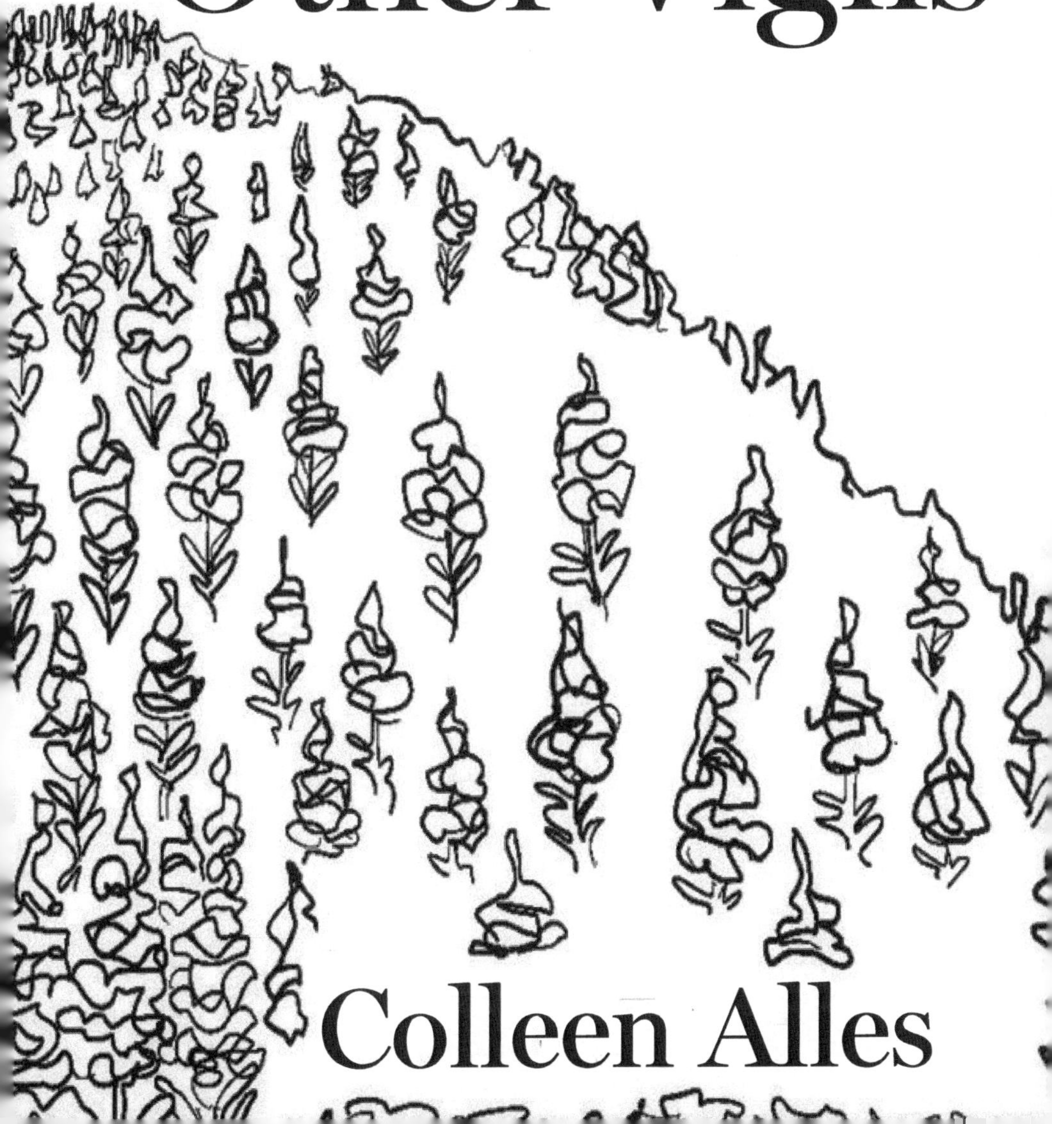

Colleen Alles

Contents

Into the Limelight

Trellis

for Mara
&
for Lincoln

Coming in from the bonfire

I'd been marveling at her for hours,
the way she let the flames lick up
her outstretched arms. The way color
seems to find her even in the dark.
The way she is so beautiful dancing
to music only she hears in her heart.

She's asleep now, my girl, so I lay down
next to the small ball of her in bed,
breathe in the smoke from the evening,
stretch wide my own wings

and remember all the moths
drawn to the bonfire tonight.

I think about how one time I read that
the real difference between butterflies and moths

is that butterflies rest with their wings closed
while moths rest with their wings
wide open.

Into the Flames

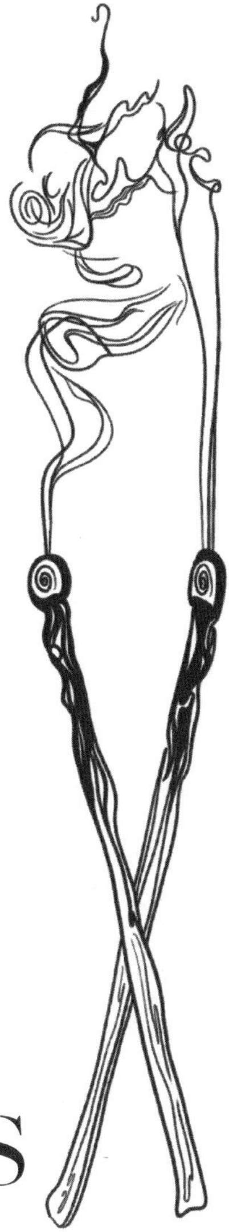

Red Sky at Morning

The opening verse
is a warning,

          a thief who might
          tell you
          ahead of time
          all the things
he's listed for the taking.

A vase,
the color of red hibiscus;
empty, yet with glass
arteries
thick like asphalt
highways

          fat with the confidence
          of where they're going.

Follow the pathways.
White dotted lines
asking to be traced.
Look toward the rust
streaking the sky.
The west is a vessel

          and

everything we've lost
everything we lose
everything we'll keep on losing

can never be painted
as arresting.

Don't take the red vase;
I've other memories
worth stealing.

Rattle

You've heard tell
of the white dove—Noah's

fearless harbinger. And too
those tales

of the clever magpie,
the bird who recalls your face.

There's the raven,
slick as pooled oil,

who remembers your every
kindness. There's less

talk of me: a stout, thick-
tailed, flightless body

a common grouse
black and tinged with red

like coals licked by fire—
a simple bird

who prefers the skin
of the Earth to the sky.

I boast few noble deeds.
I give few reasons

to think of me,
even though I keep

track of you, too:
your comings, your goings,

your feet stepping over me
as I gather a meal

from the brush.
I clock your face

too—the look in your eyes
when from behind you

I suddenly beat
my wings. When I drum.

When I rattle. When I choose
to remind you

I'm still here.

At the River

The tall reeds know what they're doing. My feet
kick the weeds as I slow from a run. I was sure

from a distance the water would still be frozen,
that the white crests in the waves would not

be in motion. But now, by the banks, I see I got it all
wrong. Mud envelopes the soles of my shoes—

maybe it wants me to stick around—and I think,
I think maybe the hardest part of losing someone

who has been so important for many years is that
this evening, there will be no one to tell this to:

the reeds, the weeds, the water flowing fast now
under bergs of ice—cold, but not cold enough

to stop moving. Even when I have little to say,
just that at the river I found a pretty place to catch

my breath. At the river I found a beautiful place
to be wrong. I wonder if the water is happy

now that it can move on. Even when I have nothing
to say, I still wish for a way you could hear it.

A Good Confidant

> *In 1638, Galileo tried a variation of Aristotle's leatherbag experiment. He constructed an apparatus consisting of a glass bulb with an airtight valve. He weighed the bulb. Next he forced air into the bulb until it contained much more than its normal volume. Now when he weighed it he found a measurable difference.*
>
> - Erik Larson, *Isaac's Storm*

By twilight, I had my heart set
on a pair of Earthly delights: the last rush

of cabernet sauvignon from the bottle
left loitering by the sink,

And an interview with a good breeze
on the back deck

Where I'd laze on my elbows,
listen to the geese warble by.
    Let out the breath I'd been holding,

And with it,
the last of the afternoon's
    secrets
    I'd been keeping.

Some of my secrets are too
sideways to set straight
    between the lines of ruled paper.
    Too unfathomable, even, for ink;

There are things I don't tell
my best friend,
the hound,
who comes sidling up beside me.

That's where the good breeze
comes in—
a gentle wind meant to listen,
then to carry my secrets away. Make

the wind
make off with a few of my better sins. Make
the wind
heavier for having talked with me.

In studying tropical storms,
their unpredictability, the wilderness
of a hurricane—

Imagine the look
in that scientist's eyes
the day he discovered

that all this air
weighs something.

Confession #68

I tell no one it was a nightmare that pulled me
from bed this morning, hours before the coffee

pot kicked on. It's February, so the dragon of my dream
was the engine of a snowplow—nothing more. Still,

that beast breathed fire on me, chased away my family.
I tell no one I still have nightmares—I am too old

for such things. Aren't I? In the worst of them, I cannot
protect you from dragons and monsters and fires—

all the worst offerings of anyone's imagination. I tell no one
at 4 a.m., while the snowplow moved up our street,

north to the lake, I was so afraid that I knelt at your bed,
trying not to touch you, my fingers icy talons. I pulled

the blankets past your chin, desperate to see your face—
desperate to put my fingers to your lips, absolutely desperate

to slow the beast inside my ribs as I see you are still breathing.

Squeal

When the garbage
truck comes
at 5 a.m.
I'm ready
in the darkness
my heartbeat hoofbeats
in my ears.
He's not coming
for me.
I close my eyes
breathe deep
try to remember
no one
is coming
for me.
No one
knows
what I've done.
I sleep with
my diary
locked under
my head.
Still.
His motor
grows closer
in the darkness.
I know I am
alone in listening
to his approach.
It's impossible
to close my eyes

again, and beyond
me to sleep.
Even as
I tell myself
the most
dangerous
secrets
are always
the ones
no one
writes down
in the first
place.

Taking out the trash

I.

I do not close the storm door gently. It's broken, it's been broken,
and when it slams against the house I'm quite happy it's busted—
just the way I feel as I twist hard at the neck of the black Hefty bag.

II.

Some people say they're mad enough to punch the wall. Not me.
I wish I was the punching kind. If you were by the trash can, I know
I'd only work a smile, ask about your day. I'd only give you more
of what you never deserved in the first place.

III.

That's what I'm thinking when I spy the large praying mantis perched
on the lid of the trashcan, frozen in the dead center. I can't move
for a long moment. She doesn't move at all.

IV.

I suppose I could fight her, push her off. I could win this standoff—
toss her to the ground. Really put her in her place. But I've already
decided it's not worth it. You're not worth it. Not anymore.

V.

I leave the trash on the lawn like a ransom. *Keep it,* I think. *Keep*
him. A female praying mantis will eat the male, I know, but as I head
back into the house, I can't in this moment recall if they do it out of instinct,
or because there's no use for the male after the deed's been done—

VI.

or if there's some other compelling reason I'm finally on the verge of understanding now.

Two swans at Reeds Lake

huddled in the snow
yesterday so close
one bird ended

where the other began, keeping
warm in late December.
Reeds Lake seemed happy

for the peace:
no kayakers, no sails.
Even the ice

fishermen with their steel
buckets are done for the year
with their tents pitched on the tundra.

And even though its edges
should bear my weight,
I held my breath

on the shoreline, considered
how most of this lake
has been lying in wait.

The deep parts need
to drop only a few more
degrees

to ice over fully.
You asked why
I ignored your message

in early November.
What no one can see
under the surface

is how every part of this body
has been ready
for the freeze.

Tell them you lost me

years back,
in the weeds, near where
the lowest branch

of that willow tree
knocked the wind
out of me.

You knifed
a curse word
in her trunk,
gashes and lines

that made
her peel in spots
where
she wasn't ready, maybe—

and sure, bark is already
dead, but I don't know

that means what
you did was right.

After, I gathered
what I could
to adorn her roots
in apology:

hewn twigs, pebbles, a couple
of cattails, cotton innards
peeling open. You had them

crumbling in your fingers, too,

and when

we heard a lone Canada
goose loud in the sky, I wanted
to ask

if you thought
she was begging her flock

to slow down,
give her a chance
to catch up,

or if she was
honking
loud and alone

so anyone listening
could keep
an invisible record
of what she was

going through.

Coax the Flame

This morning, I held a match
inside a glass jar
with an inch of candle left,
        desperate to coax the flame
        from that skinny
twig of fire
to the withered
black wick.

But that wick won't light
anymore—it's too used up—so I should

throw the candle out with the rest of the garbage.
Just a hunk of useless wax, really.
Time to let it go.

Yet instead—*instead*—I pinched
        the match in my fingers, held on
        till its tiny fire burned
        my skin. I watched

the smoke from the match
snake up in wisps. I left

that candle
        on the mantle.

And I know me
well enough
to know
        that later—tonight—

I'll find another match
somewhere in this house.

I'll light it and take it to what's left
    of that candle,
    what remains of that wick,

and—as I always seem to do—I'll find another way
to talk
myself into
trying
                again.

Matchsticks

Two of twenty are the only survivors left
in the Old Crab Steamer Okaloosa matchbook,

and they're not quite touching. Rather, they are
standing straight, as if they've been ordered. I'd only

thought I'd light a candle on the mantle, maybe
set myself up for a nice wish later. But something

about the sight of them standing by one another,
all the other matches they'd known long since

gone—Something about the way they'd probably
been keeping each other company for years

in a matchbook buried in the bottom of a drawer
changed the wish I thought I'd wish for. Gently,

I coaxed both matchsticks from the cardboard comb,
held them in my fingers together. Finally, I let them

do what they'd likely wanted to do for years,
which was (of course) to touch. For a long moment,

they rested in my palm before I struck their round
edges to the course strip on the matchbook's back.

Finally, they could fulfill their destiny; finally, they
could discover fire. Finally, they could go up in flames

together.

Narrowing

Among the new homes and mansions

Many evenings, neighbors stroll past, pointing at our curved front door, the wood-slat shutters. The roof is flat and all wrong for Michigan, they say with their eyes. We should be in Arizona, maybe California—on a sun coast, their open mouths say. We are better suited for the moon. Eventually they move on, these passersby. They don't know I watch them watch our little concrete house—a squat, confident ranch, self-assured on this block since 1945. Sometimes, after I've had red wine, I'm tempted to pad barefoot down our skinny driveway, tell everyone who stares that even in space, they'll find homes they say don't belong. They'll find other creatures they say shouldn't be there. Bet them that right now as a spaceship rubbernecks by, some alien-woman stands in her kitchen at the thick glass window, holding a big goblet of stardust in the waning light.

Seasonal Road

A few years ago,
I ran down this dirt road
all the way

to the shoreline. I ran fast
enough to keep the wind in my face.

But listen.
I'm in my forties now,
and this July

asking

my legs

to reach

the west bank

feels like
a tall order.
Even on a good day.

I slow my pace without meaning.
Each pull at the hips

becomes a battle
against humidity. Humility.

Middle age.

Two miles in, nearing a patch of tall grass
I see it:

a robin's egg—
that unmistakable shade of blue.

The egg is on the ground, cracked,
        exposed to the world. It looks too far
        from a tree to have fallen

        from a nest a mother made civilized with twigs
        and pliable branches arching in this heat.

I don't know what I expect
as I bend to look inside, but
my heart
        rate slows and there's a breath
I've been holding. I'm afraid I'll see

        a pile of bones
        or a bunch of gray feathers
        or something worse—

some sign of violence.
        A pool of yolk. I don't
know. Some evidence
a predator had its way.

But the eggshell is empty.

I study its interior. Near me,
        a rusty-throated robin

tells me to go away. It's possible
        something awful
        got to this hatchling.

Possible too, though, the wind
simply blew this empty shell

down from a nest yards away
and everything's just as

it should be. The fledgling
may be nearby

right now, quite
happy in its meanderings.

I stand up to stretch. Leave the eggshell broken
on the ground
where it lay.

My legs have little left to give, but I ask anyway.
I'm miles from home
on a seasonal road.

I have no choice
in this middle-aged body
but to believe

all broken eggs
are proof in the world

something was born
something is living
something had the strength

to fly away.

I missed the turn for the mortuary

because the train tracks
had my attention

even though no lights flashed,
no bells rang out.

I cut the radio mid-chorus—
the same song

I'd hum under my breath
at the burial.

There was no sign
of a train

or anything.
There was nothing

coming.
I turned my car around

finally found
the visitation.

I added to my apologies.
There was nothing

to say. But
there was

how long I held the phone
after the line went silent

Sunday,
when my dad called to tell me.

There is how
a dream evaporates

in the third moment of dawn.
There is how

my husband says
when I am away, the hound

sits quiet by the side door,
head cocked

at every car coming down our road.
It's not nothing–

is it? To know that?
To be told as much.

To know that
when I am away, someone

who loves me only
waits to hear

the quietest indication
I am almost home.

Looking for a lighter on my 41st birthday

They listen from the next room as I dig through the kitchen
junk drawer: screws, pens, half a dozen cords that charge God
only knows what. A rubber band older than Methuselah
snares my thumb as my husband calls, *Hon, you find one?*
I'm fishing for a book of matches in this sea of safety pins,
AAA batteries. *Why bother,* part of me wonders. Let's skip
the candle, the singing, cut the cake already. What's the point
of a candle burning barely the length of one song? I tell them
I'm coming, even though I'm no closer to the light in this rubble
of everything we needed, everything we need now, everything
we may need someday. I set aside the unticking watch I bought
in Dublin, the expired driver's license wherein I still look thin.
Here's the fortune from that one stale cookie that seemed to know
about my most recent mistake before I did. 41. Halfway there,
I think. Me. Maybe more. Maybe less. God only knows. The kids
squeal at the table. I know my husband can't keep their fingertips
from the frosting much longer. I know no one waiting for cake
is asking *Why bother?* I'm thankful, as I finally spy a Bic beneath
a book of postage stamps, that all these years, I've always been
loved enough to have lighted candles on my birthday—loved
in a way that someone's always taken a light to the tip of a wick
without worrying too much over the lifespan of my flame.

After watching the evening news

Some kind of creature makes its home
in the rotted fence boards, stacked in a thick sentry
under the back deck. I've never seen it, but I know

from the scrape of its claws, from the huff
of its breath. The beagle presses his snout
against the woodpile, desperate to catch the scent

of this thing that is alive. Each time I find
him chasing this rabbit or woodchuck
or I-pray-not a skunk, I tell the mutt

to leave well enough alone. The whatever-it-is
is no real bother to us. For years upon years,
it has nestled in the shelter of our home. This

thing that is alive has picked our deck
as the best place to hide. I tell him
on a day like today, with everything going on,

all I want is the rest of the world to return
to our little family in our little house
the same miracle of such a graceful favor.

After further consideration

I'm beginning to think our neighbor's upright
piano will not fit under the window after all
that your bottle of red would have gone better with dinner
last night, that the mailman keeps a complicated love life

or tries to. He is forever on his phone,
his smile a sideways wave crashing into his cheek
when he drops junk into our box.
He says things like *no babe, of course not babe.*

that doesn't sound like me. I'm sorry
I left you this morning for the unfurled
newspaper, the hot coffee, the pages I read
that didn't mean anything. It would have been better to stay

in our sheets, tucked in like folded laundry.
What's rare is not the litany
of chores that can always wait till later
but a summer Sunday unclaimed by plans, your skin—

a shore on which I still wish to land. That sounds
like me. Later, I say we find a real stretch of sand
wade up to our hips in Lake Michigan.
Let me make it up to you

in the middle of the waves. Let the water wash me clean.
Let the lake become my apology,
the lapping water help me say *yes babe, of course babe.*
Every single time, I was wrong to ever leave.

Modern Hardware

At the intersection
of Cottage Grove and Kalamazoo,
this Holy morning

each aisle is alive
with wall sconces
and glittering
chandeliers. I've come here

to worship at the temple
of good intentions

to see the bright wattage of all
the ways I could improve my home
if I could repent
from my lazy ways, my Earthly
procrastinations—

if I could
approach the priest
at the pulpit
passing out hammers
instead of wafers.

Look here: A dozen thick
door handles, a wall filled
with decorative knobs. A blond
saleswoman proclaims
they can be keyed
they can be catered
they can be made
to my specifications.

I could come away
from this sacred place with
brass letters for the front door,
a new mailbox
to replace ours
still dented
from our neighbor's
learning days.

There isn't any issue
this place can't fix, and as I

pass into the section
hosting simple miracles—
yard tools I didn't know existed,

I nod to the man
next to me in the aisle, wisps
of silver hair
tucked under a navy ballcap, a cane
in his right hand. I want to

commune with him
a fellow worshipper—
share the cup
the body
the blood.
There are so many things
I could ask this man
should ask him.

But when I interrupt his browsing
of all Modern Hardware
has to offer,

like a believer
astonished at the sight
of whatever may save
a wretch like me

all I manage to conjure
is *good morning, sir, please*
excuse me.

Sunday rest

All week, down the street
my neighbors have taken up
the yoke of the lawnmower

their neat square yards perfect
offerings; the kind of prayer
you can see. All this grass

is a testament to the rain
that darkened April, the storms
unrelenting. As though making

confession, Mark bows his head,
struggles the mower up a small
hill. It's my turn, I'm sure

to confess, repent. Little do they know
my conviction. At the window
I'm more lawyer than believer.

Here is the case I'll litigate,
some reasons to leave all this alone:
a pair of rabbits huddle close

in the irregular clumps by the gutter
mouths. The bees enjoy the wild
violets, a butterfly, the lone tulip

and there, by the birch, a patch of grass
so thick, a robin has found her hiding.
Sinners, we, in the throes of grass

and me, too, standing here counting
my blessings: a constellation
of fat-headed dandelions

I'm content to keep waiting.

As the potholes get filled

Let's blame the drilling
for how little I have made of today

how I mowed half the lawn
ahead of the rain

how I argued
with myself at the cupboard's top shelf

that if my kids had wanted
that Halloween candy, surely

they'd have eaten it by now.
For ten minutes, I stood

at the window, watching
the men shake in their own

sound—cacophony enough
to pull my dog from sleep.

The best of some days
is the letter I wrote

but didn't send
the Tarot card I flipped

but refused to catastrophize
the naked body I saw

in the full-length mirror
but didn't resolve

to change.
Tomorrow, when this street

goes back to being
a peaceful, noiseless dream,

perhaps I'll take the edger
to the lawn, or otherwise

remake myself into
some more useful thing.

Bird Feeder

My father curses
the fat squirrel
on the tray feeder
by the window,

whose tail sloshes,
thick like an ocean wave,
knocking
to the ground

the seeds he leaves
for his redbirds, his finches,
some jays.

A sharp rap doesn't
scare that fat rodent,
so my father pounds
the pane
with his fist.

I'm not sure if it's just
one squirrel
who visits

or a scurry,
which I learned
to be the collective
noun for squirrels.

I tell my father this,
But he is less
concerned

with the language.

Outside, he sweeps
sunflower seeds
with his fingers,
replacing the black seeds
in the bird feeder.

Then, my father returns
to the kitchen
to stand sentry

by the window, his knuckles
ready to rap

should that squirrel come back,
should a scurry come back.

I stand and watch
my father watch

and
finally—

here are the bright wings
of a cardinal.
I see him turn
his head and smile

at me—my father,
not the bird.

I am less concerned
with the bird.

I watch my father's
eyes follow
without blinking
the last thrash of scarlet

when it finally
flies away.

Garden Benediction

Ivy vines stretch
across the side yard fence, tenacious

& green—an Eden
for millipedes
earthworms, & those

little bugs
who curl into balls
when afraid. On my gentler days

I remind myself
this is not my world.

Not really. I'm only

an occasional gardener, a sometimes-
ground tender who only takes

to the roots

in desperate times. When the neighbors complain.

To all those weeds
and wildness

my steel
trowel must feel
like a foreign thing.

To all the insects
alive in the soil, this Dutch hoe

must bring

the stunning shock
of eviction. End Times.

When I finally beat
an overgrown thatch

of ragweed
there, in the dirt

I find a lightening bug
of all things.

A living thing who
like me

doesn't belong this deep
in the garden,

this far underground.

I pull her out with my trowel
          blow the dirt gently away.

          She didn't curl up into a ball.
          She didn't seem afraid.

Upon feeling the rush
of her whole world changing
she didn't

hide under the earth. She was ready

for an apocalypse, a second-coming—
anything. As subtle as I could,

I ungloved
a hand, lifted her high

on one finger. I watched her brush
off the soil

what remained of her old
way of living.

I willed my skin to whisper,
Let's see you stretch
those luminescent wings.

Wednesday Vigil

There'd been thunder enough to run
the dog in from the yard—not
only that, but to urge him
between the bedsheets,
press him
to nestle
the length of my thigh.

Under the wet fur
his skin and muscles trembled,
and I imagined he
quaked to the core—
down to the bone,
as they say.
But terror
(as it does sometimes)
had a narrowing

and now we stand
at the window
in the late afternoon. The dog follows
my gaze

to the robin reveling
in the rainwater
pooled on the sidewalk.

At this distance, I'm left
to imagine
the drops beading
on her gray feathers.

The robin stretches her wings.
We watch her give
herself a good shake.
She's found
what's good
about a storm in its wake,

and I'm left to wonder
if it's a burden to fly.

No, I decide—it wouldn't be.
From the first time she tried,
that bird took to the sky
her whole body with her.
We carry our bodies
and we do it

every day. No matter
what they weigh.
The weather rages, the world

tries to tear
the outer layers away.
Our bones are last to go. A house
inside. The bones are always home.

Earthworms

Tornado sirens
call us to the basement
after dinner. We descend

the stairs
one after another, animals
seeking shelter
underground. At least once

a summer
a thunderstorm like this

reminds us
how much light means
by revealing its absence.
When the power

gives way with a thick smack
of thunder, a wave
of heavy silence
seizes the house. The kids shriek,

crawl in the blackness on
hands and knees
across the carpet to my lap
scared but also not

scared, they inch their way
to me. My husband
flicks on a flashlight

our shadows dance
on the white cement walls. This is why

someday
when I'm not here
my kids can face any storm. That is
my hope anyway. This is why

in the morning
when we survey
the storm's damage, step over

tree limbs
in the front lawn

I'll look down
for earthworms
drowning on the sidewalk

and I'll find
not one
but four of them

fat and pink, squirming
in a puddle
scared but hopefully not
too scared

returning to the grass
together.

Heartwood

for Micah

In the dark at three a.m., I reach for your torso
when I startle from some bad dream.

Too much cheap wine, a scary movie after dinner.
Stephen King.

And my fault, too, for having gone to bed
without you. Sleep always seems to tag me first.

I peel off a bit of your outer layer, the shirt on your shoulder,
my fingers seeking the warmth of your skin. Bark

is just dead matter, meant to protect a tree—not from
nightmares, but from living fears: insects, weather, other injuries.

You're still asleep as I imagine the rings I'd see if I could
drill down to your core. More than 40 now—rings,

I mean. We are firmly middle-aged. And do you know
in the middle of any trunk lies a pillar that resists decay,

although it, like the bark, has also died away? When cut into pieces,
this part of the tree burns the longest in December fires.

Other logs haven't lasted so long.
Other fires have burned to ash more quickly.

It's the heartwood, they say—a word for the unflinching spine
of the tree.

A word for you, too, I think: the most central part of me.

Omens

Just after sunrise, I watched a blue jay push
another bird off the feeder, into a pile of leaves. I tried to recall
the meaning of seeing a blue jay. I know it's an omen for something.

Today's the last day of Leo season, and in the driveway
I tell myself that can't mean nothing. I decide later to ask the Tarot deck
for clarity. I walk my children to school, kiss them goodbye

and by the time I return to the bird feeder, I know for certain
only one thing: this morning is meant for nothing. This morning
is asking me to lose an hour to a daydream, to the imperfect

doorframe. For a while, I wander the house room to room, gathering
dirty socks for the hamper, candy wrappers for the trash. In the bathroom
mirror, I touch the low smudges that could only have come from my son.

I let his absence do some talking. Even in silence, there are signs
of life. It hits me then, in the mirror. It's the cardinal
that stands for something. A cardinal means the spirit of a loved one

who has passed away sits nearby. A blue jay doesn't mean much
of anything. In a minute I'll stand at the kettle till it whistles, pour a cup
of herbal tea. I'll remember I'm a bit of an idiot. I'll forget that, too

for a different dream. When I find the mug later cold in the kitchen
I'll take it as a good thing. I'll take a miracle for a miracle. I promised
this morning I'd do my best to stop figuring out what it all means.

Fireweed

Geography

When someone tells me
you look like me,
I think about

how the ancient glaciers
of every ice age cut channels
through mountains,
across continents,
finally settled down
as seas.

I think about how sometimes
those waters pushed land masses
away from one another—
often very far apart.

And how if you look closely
at the coastlines,
you can see
that all bodies of land

once belonged
only to
each other.

At 1:30 a.m. in the hotel, the fire alarm blares

and my first thought is not of flames, or danger. Not
even of my family, but of the ocean. I'd stayed up till mid-
night reading about the Lusitania. All those people who
thought it impossible to be hit by a U-boat's torpedo—
just like three years before, all those Titanic passengers
so confident such a ship could never sink. I tumble

from the hotel bed, my pulse exploding. The *Lusitania*
carried mostly civilians, no arms. Arms. I pluck my son
from the bottom bunk into my arms as my husband
takes our daughter from the top. We don't speak, just
find shoes, slip into the hallway where we join a throng
of fellow passengers—parents, kids in PJs. Down three

flights of stairs, I clock the brave faces all mothers
and fathers wear for their kids when something scary
happens. We're standing as a group on the grass now,
by the parking lot, but I still feel like this could be a dream.
I might be treading in the North Atlantic, and where are
the rescue boats? My son shivers. I should have grabbed

my sweater. The Lusitania sank after lunch, the Titanic
just like this in the middle of the night. Ice berg. I can't
stop picturing the bodies bobbing in the ocean, life vests
like smushed marshmallows engulfing the men, women,
children. I shudder, thinking about all the poor people
who froze in the icy Atlantic after the Titanic went down—

the poor souls lost off the southern coast of Ireland in 1915—
dark, cold, water, all around, all the confusion, all eyes
on a dark horizon. I am trying to turn my body into a life-
saving device for my son, cold against my torso, when a lady
I don't know reaches out and lays a hand gently on my shoulder.
Ma'am, she smiles. *They're saying it's okay to go back inside.*

The day after the last school shooting

My kid's with the other kids
in bright hoodies, crowding
the monkey bars. Lanky arms
and bare legs everywhere.
Like all young in the wild,
they're readying their bodies
for survival. For after I'm gone.
They slip past each other
on the wooden bridge
that sways and shakes. It takes
muscle—coordination. Work.
They aren't masterminding
like me, the fastest way out—even
here in the open. I clock every door
now, in every room. Here by the slide,
though, I scuff my feet in mud. Hold
my tongue. There's no fairness
to give them. No guarantees.
Every parent feels this, I think.
But today, we're really bearing it,
wearing collective grief
like a hair shirt. Now they swarm
by me like bees to the tire
swing—or like ants, maybe.
In the same way an ant might
leave its hill to scout for crumbs
in the woodchips or discover a sweet
thin slice of golden apple, I watch
them rush back and back and back
to one another, overflowing
with the story that there's still
something wonderful out here
everyone needs to see.

broken door

The door to my son's room won't click
into its frame no matter how hard I pull.
From the other side, my son laughs

every night I try after I tuck him in.
And I've laughed, too. Except
today, while he was in school, I was walking

by his room when the local news
started in about another school shooting
in another state, and I didn't care it was 500

miles away. I put my hand on the brass knob,
pulling till I bullied that broken door
into its frame. I pulled that door so hard

it had no choice but to click into place. It listened
to me hiss *stay put* to some wood. It ended
with me begging *stay safe where you are*

A Gull on Honeymoon

My daughter begs for the beach, which is perfectly ordinary,
except for the fact that she's never been to the beach.
The idyll of the right day hasn't yet hit this summer.

Also, I'm scared.

The endless high wave warnings
for Lake Michigan shuck our faces from
the evening news at each account of a drowning.

Still, here she is, all dimples and brown barrel curls.
She's holding her swimsuit—the one with pink polka dots.
She's hard to turn down, so I find myself asking my body
for yet another favor:

that my limbs will bend and buoy in Lake Michigan
for as long as my daughter wants to shriek and laugh
among the waves, a gull on honeymoon with fresh
water. I wrap her in my long arms, my skin sighing relief,

and each time she digs her small talons into my shoulders,
it's a promise we make to each other
to not let go.

Interurban Trail

Early Sunday, I catch sight
of a big man bent

at the waist by the bramblebush
as I round a familiar bend. I force

my legs to a faster clip,
turn this trail into a war

path. I am water
coming to boil

in the kitchen's kettle,
too angry

not to whistle out loud. He looks
up as I rush pass, his face

a flat map of confusion.
He was studying deer tracks,

I realize. He was holding
a magnifying glass. I read

this whole thing wrong. He was never
any danger. This was only

my ready, roiling anger.
Still, I keep up this new pace

as I put another mile between us.
I'm a woman running alone

in the woods, leaving footprints
in the mud. There's no one

around to say next time,
this doesn't go the other way.

Signpost

When we are lost in the woods the sight of a signpost is a great matter.
-C.S. Lewis, *Surprised by Joy*

First, I tripped in the courtyard—not
even on the uneven paver stones
or the treacherous roots skimming
under fallen leaves like snakes
at the wake of the water—not

even because of the sloping dirt hill
among the goldenrod and toad-brown trees,
but of all things at the feeling
I've been here before. Once, at least.

This reed-lined pond, these water lilies.
I'd known these patches of mud
dirty in their jubilee. Without a signpost,
I could not be sure. Without a better memory,
I could not parse out what had happened

from what I dreamed, sort out the impasse
that swirled inside of me. Later on, by the maple trees
when I thought my feet were out to get me,
I found a swath of branches
too familiar for this to be our first meeting.

You turned around, laughing as I stood up.
Of much less importance was every memory
before this afternoon, these woods—every
half-brained dreamy wondering
giddy in the harboring—even

the sometimes-pressing notion
that tells me someday
I'll be yours for the leaving.

Piano Lesson

My mother pays the tight-lipped piano
teacher to come over once a week.
Wednesdays at four, I make room for her

on the narrow bench. She makes me
sorry I do not practice more. I should have
Greensleeves down by now. I want

to tell her I'm astonished by the bass clef:
I've never seen a broken chord before.
Arpeggio, she corrects me. A chord I will play

one note at a time. A chord that climbs
and comes back down, climbs
and comes back down again.

It isn't that hard. But the broken chords fall
apart in my left hand, slippery as a bar of soap
in the bath. I am ready to cry. I only want

chords that are stacked in neat lines
ready at first sight. I want all of them to look
like what they are. But my teacher

and her expectant face have no mercy for me.
C, E, G, E, C. C, E, G, E, C. Get used to it
she says. *Arpeggios are everywhere.*

Silviculture

After the last bell, my daughter lingers
by the large maple shading the sand

near the swing set. A thunderstorm
blew through our block last night

leaving half a dozen branches
abandoned on the grass. I don't

know why she's gathered
them until she begins

replanting the twigs upright
in the sand in such careful mounds.

Later, when she asks how tall
those trees she planted will grow

I don't tell her it's not
gonna work. The wind will

blow them over, or they won't get
enough sun or water to root

through sand. I don't
tell her those branches will

wither, die, that the maple
herself is slowly dying

even in the bright & wild
joy of our extraordinary living

so we leave the playground
side by side & I just say

oh, babe we're all gonna grow
very, very tall.

Watching my daughter study the chessboard

her bangs hang over her eyes.
She favors the knight–
the only one who can jump

over other pieces. She wishes
the bishop could move
from a light path to a dark.

The pawns are always
in her way. When I tell her
the lynchpin of the whole game–

a crowned man–can only move one
square at a time, she frowns
over the rim of her glasses till

I'm laughing. I don't go easy
on her like I used to, but I say
it's a hard game. My dad taught me

when I was her age. I can picture
his tan and white wooden board,
its uniformity. I can hear my dad

whistling Neil Diamond, Lionel
Ritchie. I show her consequences
of her moves but let her make

decisions anyway. There's a moment
I could take her queen, but I pretend
not to see. Maybe I am still going

easy. I don't mind. I call it a draw
when it's dinnertime, shaking her hand
the way my dad did mine. Before she

sets the table, I ask her to put the game
away, remembering as she does my dad's
set, much nicer than mine: places for each

piece carved in green foam, the way he held
each ceramic piece for a moment before
it went to where it belonged. The way

he made order from the chaos after every
game. From the chaos of most things.
His smile each time he told me, *good game.*

Thursday Night at Great Clips

for Mara

These days, my daughter cares for nothing
but the moon. Her whispers wax and wane.
At breakfast, we're in phases; at dinner,
we eclipse. By bedtime, she insists a story
shouldn't end without a moon. On Thursday,

she gets her hair cut—a little overdue.
In the mirror, I watch her face grow round
as crescents of curls fall to the ground.
For a moment, I gaze as she appraises herself:
new hair, new face. In a bob, my daughter

looks less like the girl I used to hoist
on my shoulders—even less like the girl I wish
would never grow older. As I pay at the register,
she plucks a pink sucker from the countertop
bouquet. If love ever chose a sound, I think

it'd be my daughter's name. *Hey Mom,* she says
once we're back in the van. Sticky candy orbits
her face. *Did you know the moon doesn't*
make light of its own? It all comes from the sun.
Moons just do what suns do in the first place.

Flu Shot at Walgreens

There are things we do not say
the young pharmacy tech and me

He takes me to a special room
I roll up my sleeve as far as I can

He hands me a clipboard to initial
busies his hands with the needle

Even with the mask covering
his nose and mouth

I can tell I have some years
on him but bless his heart he flirts

with me anyway
tries to or starts to maybe

makes a joke about Michigan winters
how he's ready to break up with them

for the call of California
her warmth, her sun, her holiday season

with no snow to be shoveled
It's the week before Thanksgiving

I am just now learning how to live
the years of my life where I am old enough

to be some man's mother
I really might be old enough to be his

Maybe not
It's hard

to peg his age but as I hand the clipboard back
my years as a number stare up at us

He hates this job
Eighteen months in and he's ready

to forget the florescent lights
the prescriptions the headaches

the health insurance the hassles
On the west coast he will be a bartender

One type of medicine for another
I joke as he rubs

a cold circle of alcohol on my skin
Yes that's right he laughs

This might sting
and I say after two babies

I have greatly reconsidered what I call pain
He grins *Mad respect*

I say before I forget
let me tell you good luck

in California
I wish you

All the best
He smiles a smile I can't see under his mask

I only see its evidence
in the parentheses of skin

huddling around his eyes
I wish you the best too he says

although I am a woman with fewer
adventures ahead

He pricks at my shoulder
I feel the sting and then his fingers as he rubs

at the bright bloom of blood
with a cotton swab

with the kind of tenderness
I wish I had told him reminded me

in a way of all the best parts
of being a mother.

Immortal Jellyfish

In one of your books,
we read about jellyfish.

Immortal jellyfish
can live forever

because they revert
to earlier stages of life

when they encounter stress.
They *regenerate,* more or less.

I don't read those last parts
because I don't know how

to explain regenerate.
I think I just want you

to know that some things
that live *do* live forever;

I'm not sure I knew that—
not sure I'd given any

thought to immortal jellyfish
before today. Yet now they're all

I seem to think about. Immortal
jellyfish catapult

to become the most important
animal. Immortal

jellyfish are now
the only thing

I hope you remember
about this day.

January 1st

for Lincoln

It takes a moment to buoy from a dream.
You crawl into my bed; I pull the quilt
over your shoulders. You nestle next to me.

Lavender floats from your hair; my lips brush
your spiral curls, then the doughy arc of your cheek.
You'll turn five this year. It seems like a certainty.

In the dark, you smile; you look so proud to have
found me. Pulling you close, I imagine a tiny boat
curling up to a dock. Boats need a sturdy place

when they're ready to come in from the sea. We are
a small body by a big body. When you sigh, it's me
forgiving my big body for its rickety boards, its soggy

posts, its broken places, a host of imperfections. Now,
at dawn, the start of a new year, it's hard to believe
there was ever a notion to change this. Yes. In my mind,

I am already rewriting last night's resolutions.

Into The Limelight

Upstream

If I say *think of a river*
and your mind
sparks alive
with the image of water

tightening a hairpin turn
so rough the waves cap
furious white at the top
it might be time

to take yourself
away from these worries
find a quiet square of land
take a long walk alone

as best you can. Listen
to the evening train
study all the weathervanes
any harbinger

of the burgeoning fall.
Step until the waters
are smooth. I know
you've heard you'll get over

this soon, that there are plenty
of fish in the sea. Speaking
of rivers, speaking of fish
it's unlikely they feel heartbreak

but I like to think
there are certain parts of any river
even the most stoic of salmon
refuse to ever cross again.

Lime Lake, July 4

Flat-eyed minnows zip & skitter,
evading my daughter's gauzy net
suffocating as a wedding veil.

Hours ago, after breakfast
by the long dock, she found a baby
snapping turtle

named it Frank
of all things. Frank (I didn't tell her)
is the name of a guy

a friend of mine
once set me up with for a hopeful
date. He took me

to a baseball game.
Frank drank draft beer slow, insisted
each inning he needed

to explain the score. He didn't
see above my chin. There was no
second date.

I told my daughter Frank
was the perfect
name for this small reptile

cold-blooded & hard-
shelled, so content
to be confined to a casserole dish—

a 9 x 13 glass
terrarium filled with rocks & blades
of grass & water. He ate

a dozen caught minnows, one
at a time, his black tongue
always lolling.

Part of me wanted to ask
if he remembered me, too—
that kiss he made me say yes to

as he dropped me off, his lips scaly
on my cheek. But Frank's dull
eyes gave me nothing:

no spark of memory.
When the fireworks began, I told
my daughter

it was time to set the turtle
free. I'd like to say
he jumped grateful

& gleeful from that gray rock, that he
headed straight & brave
for the lake's middle, lighted

by a burst of light
over the quiet waves—that he left me
too, a sign of understanding

or repentance
in his wake.
But I don't think that's the case.

All these years later, Frank is a reptile
easing himself, alone, into
the shallowest part of the lake.

Midwest Nice

Over the fence, Rebecca waves,
asks if we've heard their chickens.

They're new. When I say we haven't,
the rush of eyebrow to hairline

tells me I've erred. *Really,* she says.
Not at peep. I don't know why

I've doubled down. Maybe because
I want to believe she can't hear *my* yard,

my house—all the times I've screamed
at the kids, cursed the dog. Perhaps

because last spring I caught her husband
at the sliding door in his underwear,

his belly pale and round as a cantaloupe.
Perhaps there's no cap on Midwest nice—

the way we hold court on the weather, make
talk in any grocery line. How we stand

in the sun talking about something when
we have little to say. Rebecca wipes

her forehead, says *that's great,* asks
after our summer plans. Suddenly, the dog

stiffens at my side. His ears shoot up,
he throws back his head in a howl. In all

the years we've been neighbors,
they've never complained about a hound

in the city. *Oh,* I say, *You know what?*
I think I hear them now.

How strangers in Michigan say I love you in a snowstorm

one that sends you out
for bread and milk and eggs,
and okay, a bottle of wine too,
plus batteries, since you'll be
in for days

when a kind man waves you
ahead in line to pay, even though he
only has beer and laundry detergent,
he insists, and then as you head
out of the store with your bags
braced for the storm
he catches your eye, nods his head,
raises a wide smile and says,

"You drive safe."

Condolences for Bill

Mostly, we just yelled *hi* from across the street
or I'd give her a smile, shrug as my hound
took a piss on your lawn. *He's cute but dumb,*
I'd tell her. *My apologies.* She would laugh.

It was as much her habit as it still is yours
to sit on your front porch rocking, smoking,
cancer aside. Your wife, as you know, was slight
in stature. Sometimes I wouldn't see her at first—

a woman wilting into her bones, her body
shrinking, steadily, receding to its first home
a little more each time I saw it. And every evening
when I reached my side door, the beagle exhausted

on the leash, panting at my feet, but pleased
I'd indulged him the excursion—before I let him
off the lead I made sure to glance her way, made certain
I held up one hand for a long, final waving.

Family Tree

The neighbors kindly do not mention the raw intimacy
of our bushes. The two shrub clumps were meant to mark
boundaries, to subtly separate our yard from theirs. Then one
April, the brambles fell in love. What began as a curious,
innocent extension of leaves became an obsessive need
to invade, to intertwine, to erase all space between.

When holding the pruning shears, I did not have the heart
to impose after all, just as after my son was born, I stopped
pulling up dandelions and Scotch thistle by the roots.
To me, they were now orphaned, willful plants who
only wanted a chance to stand by something as effortlessly
vibrant as a sunflower, an orchid, a rash of bright red roses.

On Killing Spiders

In my haste to return from the kitchen,
I nearly drop the pint glass I pinched
from a Dublin bar when I was twenty

and wandering around
the part of my life where
taking things that didn't belong to me

felt like the right way to prove
I was living. Now, I use that pint
glass to catch spiders,

slipping stiff junk
mail underneath. I usher
wanderers outside. But as I hear

the thump of some plastic toy heavy on
my son's bedroom floor, I worry I am
too late to give this spider back

to December. I'd wanted to teach
my son how to do this, show him
there's always a moment to help

another life with its living. In his room
though, I see it—the spider, moving,
unkilled after all. I am careful

not to catch a hair-thin leg
with the glass's lip—careful to ease
the little spider into this cloudy dome

from far away, from another
me altogether, and then to the back
deck. The spider disappears in seconds.

My son and I shiver. We steal
inside, and I keep wandering the part
of my life vivid with second chances.

Laundry

You haven't done this to me in months:
woken me in the exact middle of the night.

I heard you crying, crept to your room.
I rocked you as though we were slow dancing
to an unheard, invisible song.

Your hands tighten on my shoulder and I find
I don't exactly mind the interruption from sleep,
the excuse to sway with you.

And I don't even mind the middle-of-the-night thoughts
that now slip into my mind, like a pile
of dirty laundry demanding to be dealt with.

I squeeze you close, because
what if you were pulled from a dream
by a middle-of-the-night thought
like this one:

Someday, when all our nights and days are done,
how will our two souls know one another?
Will they have to work hard to find each other?

And when they reunite, will it feel just as wonderful
as this exact moment—

your gentle breath on my cheek, your tiny sigh.

Will it feel like summer sunshine,
          like clean sheets?

What about this, Baby:

Maybe we will feel like two matching socks,
separated once,
cycled apart for a time,

but eventually paired together again,
folded into each other, and
gently laid down as one.

Ordinary Inning

I.

A radio atop the beer fridge
in the back of the garage
keeps my father company.

The D.J. slings some
10 a.m. trivia: a verbal Rubik's cube.

First player, fastest player, best player.
To some.

My father paces—slow steps, long
swigs, repairing a broken lawn mower.
My whole life, there is
nothing
he can't fix.

II.

Many years later, I stand
on a diamond in Mississippi
where the locals tell me

a batter can muscle
a pitcher's hurl all the way
into the next county.
Quite a miracle.

I imagine
my father here, wish him
with me. He would humbly love
this muddy outfield, this
humid, Spring evening.

I imagine
    an ordinary inning here.

And I imagine my father
    after hours of listening to callers' clumsy swings,
    all the wrong answers, setting down his can,
    combing the back of his brilliant mind,
    finally dialing the trivia line.

Woman in House

When I dream of my mother,
it is my bad conscience
surfacing.

That's what my dream dictionary
tells me.

She spoke to me
in my dream last night,
but you know
as well as I
how impossible it is to understand
what
mothers
and
figures
and lovers
and anyone else is trying to
say to us in our dreams.

It is as though their messages are spoken
backward or upside down,
from an ancient age.

Do you know what she
was trying to tell me?

Whatever it was,
she smiled
and laughed and
her laughter woke me,
uncovered me,
made me thumb once again through
that big book of symbols
looking for her in
any page I can.

How to thank an early memory

On the back porch, a rickety
screen door creaked and moaned
in every thunderstorm. The latch

had long ago given out, so even
an evening breeze could slam
that door back into its frame.

And the bang that sometimes
shook the house
when I was a girl

sent my mother's hand sailing
straight over her heart,
then to her lips

as she stifled the rupture
of a sudden belly laugh,
and so I grew up thinking

that our old screen door
didn't really need fixing,
no matter what my mother said.

Trellis

The funny thing about stories

He was skinny & scared—the puppy I brought home
that November from the animal shelter. I learned he liked
to chase long-eared rabbits in the backyard

to the loose-board corner of the fence. The rabbits
always outran him. I'd tell him he was a good boy anyway.
And when he was an old dog, I stood

on the deck one twilight & caught him chasing
a gray rabbit—watched his mouth go around
the animal's skinny neck. Later that night, I thought—

of all things—about something I once heard at a loud
garden party: that in a story, the reader cares most
about whomever she meets first. The character

who greets us is the one who wins our sympathies.
Because this story began with an orphaned, underweight
dog, right now, you might be rooting

for the beagle who finally got his way. But if I could
go back, start this whole thing over, I might begin
with the rabbit, downy soft & searching for clover in the weeds.

Then, you might be pleased to hear that when he took
that rabbit in his powerful teeth, I yelled Charlie's name loud
from the back deck, & he dropped the rabbit instantly.

The night air swelled with the mournful notes of a beagle's bay.
Astounded, Charlie & I watched the hero of the story run away.

Epiphany

I swear I feel you take my arm
downtown as we leave the bar,
swear you are about to kiss me.
Instead, you point us to the life-

size nativity outside city hall.
The usual three, plus a shepherd
with a wooden crook, wisemen
with wistful looks. I wish not

for the first time the wine would say
what I can't. You wonder how much
all these figures weigh. I ask, *Do you*
think she told him right away?

Mary, I mean. Joseph. About the baby,
the angel—everything? For a moment
you shine back at me. I wonder
if it's miracle time. I wonder

if you finally see me. I think I feel
you bending in but I'm wrong. Mistaken
at least. You crouch down to baby Jesus,
brush some snow off his manger. You

laugh and say, *Please—that man was so*
in love, he was ready to believe anything.

Teen Years

In the northeast corner of
    her garden

and for ten thankless years

my mother anchored peony
    bushes with stakes and cages

so her flowers
would stand straight and tall
in early June

when they were finally ready

to leave the tight balls
of their buds

when they were finally open

to holding the overwhelming
weight of
their own
magnificent blooms.

St. Thomas, the U.S. Virgin Islands

on the mug I chose
from your cupboard

while you showered
this morning.

Cartoon tourists in bikinis
a thick yellow line

of sand parallel with the sky.
Someone must have gone—

an old girlfriend
maybe. She thought of you

in some strip mall
amidst the powerful

disorientation of travel.
I hear you cursing—you

dropped the shampoo.
I get a slim glimpse

at your torso through
the vertical slat

a door makes when it
inches away

from its own frame.
And I am remembering

my mother in this interstice:
a long time

ago on a summer vacation.
From the edge of our hotel

bed I studied her as she
emerged from the large white tub

wet hair clinging
to patches of sunburn

on her back. I watched her dry
her body with her back to me

watched her lay the starched
white towel across her

shoulders like angel wings.
She gave me a smile

I didn't understand then
but I think I do now

as she put on her robe
widening the door

just enough to let me in
telling me it was my turn now.

Close of the Day

After Rene Magritte's, *The Empire of Light*

Like an eavesdropper
on a low conversation
in another room,

a lamppost stands alone
outside the walls of the white stone
house—the one shuttered

to the world, closed in a tight
cocoon refusing entry to further
light. Upstairs, the house

seems content to let the twin
windowpanes speak
for themselves, mark

the telltale sign
of a couple up
past their bedtime.

A man too restless to sleep,
a woman too tired
from the long walk

under the hemlock
for dreams. Their bodies
hum from mulled wine

warmed on the stove:
redness and richness
honey and tangerine

basking in their own
remnants, the close of the day
so in love with its own

bright spices.

Preparing for the dinner

to be served at seven
my mother skins russet potatoes

lets their oblong slices
rain into the sink

I take another sip
of table wine

press on her again
an offer to peel.

She smiles. There's something
else I want to say

but her hands have moved on
to the pie

my lips to wine
and how is it we arrange

the right words anyway?
I want to tell her

she's always made everything
look easy

but I think she'll think
I mean Thanksgiving

when I mean
everything. I mean

the sum
of all the years. I mean

her kindness, her
laughter. I mean

the jewelry box
she let me keep.

How she'd hold my hand all the way
through a movie. I mean

a hundred things I can't say. Isn't
every family this way?

I set the table. I pour
more wine.

I say thank you
for having us.

I say thank you
when she hands

over yeast rolls.
She says thank you

for setting the table.
She says thank you

when I pour her a glass
of wine.

She folds her hands
for the blessing.

I say thank you
after dessert

but it’s not what I mean.
I don’t mean

pecan pie. I don’t
mean coffee with cream

the fullness of our bellies
or the wonder of this feast.

I mean
I don’t know who I would be

if she wasn’t such
a masterpiece.

Relic

for Garrett Stack

Late July is a lousy time to tear down a fence
but a pair of shirtless young men take their tools

to the rotting boards anyway, wicking sweat
from their foreheads, spitting intermittently,

blasting country ballads from a boombox
they somehow knew I wouldn't mind. Yes, I did

watch for a time, but I don't mean it like that.
I waited for a break to bring ice water,

thinking of my husband: how he milked cows
alongside his father at four in the morning—

the most faithless hour. Not hot work like this,
but hard just the same. They thanked me

then piled more fence boards on the flatbed.
That fence should have come down

a decade ago, but we'd always been too polite
to say so. After they left, the dog and I ambled

outside. I pinched a stray nail from the ground.
And here is where I could lie, say

I forgot his weathered leash, but the truth is
I wanted him to run free into this new expanse.

He's lived all his life with that eyesore. Now
he's whipping his tail like a metronome, telling me

it's okay it was long overdue. He's telling me
it's never too late for something to become new.

An apology to Bertha Mason, first wife of Edward Rochester

We were gone all Saturday. I was eight, maybe
nine. It was late August. The fair was in town
and demanded everything else be forgotten except
the Gravitron, the Alpine Peaks, Elephant Ears, the tickets
my sister tucked into the back pocket of her jeans.
The Ferris Wheel let us look at car roofs
in the parking lot. We won a goldfish at a booth
with the pop of a balloon, a dart whisked
from my sister's right wrist. We hadn't tried to.
There had been no plan for that fish. We took it home
in a Ziplock bag, put it in a mason jar. Tomorrow
we'd buy fish flakes. Tomorrow, we'd buy a real tank.
Tomorrow we'd settle on a name. The Ferris Wheel
beckoned us back. We didn't leave until sweat
dried in streaks on our skin. The next morning, before
we could beg for money and a ride to the store, we checked
on the fish in the living room. But the mason jar was empty.
My sister dropped to her knees, reaching among the red
tassels of the rug. She shrieked when she found it
eyes forever open, mouth agape in a scream.
It didn't make any sense for a second. The prize
we left unnamed with no food, alone for too long
in a jar that was too small had jumped out. I'm sorry
it took me so long to understand what had happened.

And then why.

Mad Dogs on the wall

After Jack Vettriano's, *Mad Dogs*

My daughter sees me

on the beach,
under an umbrella,
holding my hemline

from the waves,
the wet sand.

There's a man nearby,
and far off, a blue

line on the horizon daring
the sky alone to meet it.

That's you, she says.
Which one? I ask, though

of course it's the wrong
way to respond.
I am

neither woman
in this painting,
and I could have just
said that—
should have just said that—

should have told her
        straight away

that although
my dark hair is often
        pulled into a bun
        to keep it out of the way,

and

although in Michigan
we talk constantly
        of the beach and little else
        in good weather,
        I say nothing.

I am caught that
to her, I might be
        a faceless woman
        wasting a summer afternoon,

leaving
deep grooves
        in the sand
        behind her
        as she goes.

I am caught that
to her, this picture
        on the wall might be

        a photograph of some
adventure from my life—

some memory
I've thought enough of
    to have captured,
    framed,
    hung above my dresser

but have not yet found
the right moment
to share

    with her.

When She Leaves Us for Paris

it will be
my fault.
I hung
sketches
of street scenes
above her pillow,
the Eiffel Tower
its own beacon
in the dark.
I sang her
alouette, gentille alouette,
then let
my eyes widen with talk
of the Seine.
I whispered
of Notre-Dame at night.
I let her
taste my wine.
I braided butterflies
in her curls,
made her
a bed of rose petals
and pearls.

And I'll remember
even back then,
her prayers read like
lists, and
even back then,
she skipped rocks
in her dreams,

into oceans and rivers
and ponds and streams,
already half
a world
away.

Acknowledgements

I am grateful to be a writer with so many supportive people in my life.

Thank you Garrett Stack for reviewing early drafts of many of these poems and for saying such kind things about the book. Thank you to my first mentor at Spalding University, Kathleen Driskell, who helped me rethink and revise many of these poems. Thank you Douglas Manuel, Lynnell Edwards, Karen Mann, and all my writer-friends at Spalding University. In particular, thank you Thursday morning poets: Abbie Rudibaugh, Jo Tyler, Joan McBride, Katie Massa Kennedy, Maud Welch, and Melanie Weldon-Soiset; our weekly check-ins help me practice writing more thoughtfully and intentionally.

Thank you Nicole Birkett, Barry Matthews, and all my Ludington Writer friends! You all are wonderful. Thank you to Anita Skeen, Jared Morningstar, and the amazing folks with Friends of Theodore Roethke. Thank you Kristin Brace, Phillip Sterling, Caitlin Cowan, and Linda Nemec Foster for being kick-ass companions on the journey. Thank you Norman Belanger and Megan Turner for being such wonderful writers and friends.

Thank you Anne-Marie Oomen, Dave Harrity, and Emily Stoddard for saying such kind things about the book, too!

A gigantic thanks to Paul Albano, Skyla Pearson, and the incredible team at Red Rook Press! This book was in such wonderful hands with you. Thank you Olabayo Awodirepo, Wrenley Brown, Jane Champ-O'Connell, Alyssa Heitz, Abbey Hightower, Jordana Kinder, Quade Mainzer, Kylie Miller, Anna Kate Moorer, and Marin Poleshek.

Lastly, thank you to my friends and family. A lot of

evidence suggests being friends with a creative writer (or living with one) is not easy, but you all surround me with so much love and you make it look easy. No one's got it down like Micah Alles.

Gratefully acknowledged are the publishers and editors of the following magazines, journals, books, and anthologies where many of these poems first appeared:

Coming in from the bonfire originally appeared in *The Michigan Poet*, Summer 2020.

At the River originally appeared in *The Orchards Poetry Journal*, June 2022.

A Good Confidant originally appeared in *Peninsula Poets*, Poetry Society of Michigan, Spring Issue 2022: Volume 79-1.

Confession #68 originally appeared in *Making Waves: A West Michigan Review*. Volume 2, Fall 2022.

Taking out the trash originally appeared in *New Note Poetry*, Winter 2022 issue. January 2023.

Two swans at Reeds Lake originally appeared in *The Orchards Poetry Journal*, Winter 2023, and received second place in Nymeria Publishing's December 2023 contest for long-form poems (theme: goodbye).
Coax the Flame originally appeared in *Making Waves: A West Michigan Review*. Volume 2, Fall 2022.

Seasonal Road originally appeared in the anthology *Angels on a Sylvan Road: An Anthological Ode to the Natural World*. MyrtleHaus Publishing: March 2024.

Looking for a lighter on my 41st birthday originally appeared in *Hearth & Coffin,* Volume 3, Issue 4. January 8, 2024 (theme: burn).

Sunday rest originally appeared in *Qua Literary and Fine Arts Magazine,* Winter 2023.

Bird Feeder originally appeared in the chapbook *So What to Say to a Bird.* Celery City Press, February 2021.

Garden Benediction and *Wednesday Vigil* originally appeared in the anthology *Angels on a Sylvan Road: An Anthological Ode to the Natural World.* MyrtleHaus Publishing: March 2024.

Geography originally appeared in the chapbook *Induction: poems for my new daughter.* Finishing Line Press, 2018.

The day after the last school shooting originally appeared in *Last Stanza Poetry Journal,* Issue #13: These Things We Carry, July 2023.

A *Gull on Honeymoon* originally appeared in the chapbook *So What to Say to a Bird.* Celery City Press, February 2021.

Piano Lesson originally appeared in *Peninsula Poets,* Poetry Society of Michigan, Spring Issue 2023: Volume 80-1.

Silviculture originally appeared in *Tar River Poetry,* Spring 2023.

Thursday Night at Great Clips originally appeared in *The Orchards Poetry Journal,* Winter 2023.

Flu Shot at Walgreens originally appeared in *Qua Literary and Fine Arts Magazine,* Winter 2023.

How strangers in Michigan say I love you in a snowstorm originally appeared in *Michigan Roots: A Poetry Society of Michigan Anthology*. August 28, 2021.

Family Tree originally appeared in *Mothers Always Write,* February 24, 2020.

Laundry originally appeared in the chapbook *Induction: poems for my new daughter*. Finishing Line Press, 2018.

Ordinary Inning originally appeared in *The Twin Bill,* Issue 13: October 27, 2023.

Woman in House originally appeared in the chapbook *Porch Light to the Longshoreman*. Finishing Line Press, 2019.

Teen Years originally appeared in *Iris Farm and Letters* as the third-place winner in the 7th annual Lavender Farm Annual Poetry Contest, Summer 2022.

St. Thomas, the U.S. Virgin Islands originally appeared in *Making Waves: a West Michigan Review*. Fall 2023.

Close of the Day originally appeared in *Paper Dragon,* Volume 5: Summer 2023.

Relic originally appeared in *Iris Farm and Letters* as the second-place winner in the 8th annual Lavender Farm Annual Poetry Contest, Summer 2023.

An apology to Bertha Mason originally appeared in the anthology *The Power of the Feminine "I"*, Volume II. January 2024.

Mad Dogs on the wall originally appeared in *Among the Happy Poets: Theodore Roethke's Influence in a Time of Disruption*. Spring 2022.

When She Leaves Us for Paris originally appeared in the chapbook, *So What to Say to a Bird*. Celery City Press, February 2021.

Among the new homes and mansions originally appeared in *Peninsula Poets, Poetry Society of Michigan*, Spring Issue 2024: Volume 81-1.

About the Author

Colleen Alles is a writer, librarian, and Michigander for life. The author of two novels and a full-length poetry collection, Colleen works as a developmental editor and serves as a contributing editor (short fiction) at *Barren Magazine*. When she isn't reading or writing, Colleen enjoys distance running and spending time with her family, including a well-loved beagle, Charlie. You can find her online at www.colleenalles.com.

About the artists

DeAndra Gauntt was born and raised in Montgomery, Alabama and is an undergraduate student at the University of Alabama. She is pursuing a BFA in Interdisciplinary Studies with a focus on Art Business. DeAndra's specialty lies in digital illustrations, focusing on character and environment storytelling, while also engaging in prose writing in the fantasy, science-fiction, drama, and romance genres. Much of her artwork and writing focuses on providing Black American representation in genres in which minorities are often underrepresented. In her free time, she enjoys sewing, reading, crafting, playing her favorite video games, and watching other people play her favorite video games.

•"Into the Flames" •"Into the Limelight"

Elizabeth Golembiewski grew up in Fenton, Michigan and is now a BFA Studio Art student at the University of Alabama. She concentrates in drawing and digital media, but she's also developing her skills as a sculptor. She prefers media such as pastels, bronze, and sticky tabs, where she can build up layers of rough texture. Impressionist art is one of her larger influences.

•"Trellis"

Anna Luis is a creative media, English, history, and theatre major from South Carolina who is also working towards her MBA. She thrives on engaging with her diverse interests by creating in many mediums and can most often be found hanging around rescued street dogs. She plans to create films and television as a career. Vegan. Sleeps with the light on.

•Cover •"Narrowing"

Anna White is an avid reader of poetry and fantasy works, with some of her favorites being Julie Kagawa's *Blood of Eden* series and various collections of folklore, classic fairy tales, and mythology. She loves to pet moss, and, similarly to certain birds, she adores shiny objects and things that go clink. Anna's life dream is to live in a cryptic yet luxurious cave with lots of beanbags, books, and RPG video games, of which Skyrim and Red Dead Redemption 2 are her all-time favorites.

•"Fireweed"

Red Rook Staff

Red Rook Press is a student-run literary press from the University of Alabama.

Acquisitions

Anna Kate Moorer (liaison), Anna Kate Baxter, Jane Champ-O'Connell, Claire Duke, Hannah French, Camryn Haag, Angie Henle, Aric Huffman, Sydney Jason, Vivian Johnson, Meghen Kellem, Alaina Kelley, McKenzie Knight, Olivia LaRose, Cassie Montgomery, Chance Phillips, Marin Poleshek, Erin See, Jordan Steele, John Underwood, Alyssa Walker, Alyssa Wallner

Audio

McKenzie Knight, Jordan Steele, Ever Wood

Editing

- Skyla Pearson (liaison), Olabayo Awodirepo, Wrenley Brown, Jane Champ-O'Connell, Alyssa Heitz, Abbey Hightower, Jordana Kinder, Quade Mainzer, Kylie Miller, Anna Kate Moorer, Marin Poleshek

Design and Production

DeAndra Gauntt (liaison), Angie Henle, Addie Dobereiner, Michael Esparza, Hannah French, Ainsley Greer, Elizabeth Golembiewski, Anna Luis, Jordan Steele, Anna White

Promotions and Outreach

Maya Mungo (liaison), Martin Albright, Anna Kate Baxter, Camryn Haag, Sarah Vance Harrison, Kelsie Jackson, Jordana Kinder, Morinsola Kukoyi, Reese Johnson, Nic Lowery, Hannah Mauck, Cassie Montgomery, Jesse Mullins, Averi O'Brien, Erin See, Jordan Steele

Website Design and Content

Nic Lowery (liaison), Autumn Carpenter, Hayley Green, Aric Huffman, Meghan Kellem, McKenzie Knight, Anna Luis, Jesse Mullins, Ansel Smith, Jordan Steele

Faculty Advisers

Paul Albano, Merrill Lee Girardeau, Stephanie Marker, Jane Morton, Travis Turner

Note on Typography

This book is set in Mauritius, the last font created by German designer Georg Trump. Due to the printing industry's shift towards cold type technology, the font was largely overlooked, and its home foundry closed down. However, designer Patrick Griffin expanded and modernized the typeface for digital use in 2013, preserving its original spikiness and unique spacing while adjusting peculiarities caused by its original metal-type nature.